MW00787244

BLOWN WIDE OPEN

A Collection of Holidays

SALVADORE POE

Transcribed and edited by
Seth Colby and Vanya Green

Liberation IS Publishing

Blown Wide Open, A Collection of Holidays

www.liberationis.com www.salvadorepoe.com

Published by: Liberation IS Publishing

Copyright © 2020 Salvadore Poe DiBartolo, USA

All rights reserved. No part of this book may be reprinted or reproduced or utilized in any form or by any electronic, mechanical, or other means, now known or hereafter invented, including photocopying and recording, or in information storage or retrieval systems, without permission in writing from the author.

Paperback

ISBN-10

1732141142

ISBN-13

9781732141148

ePub/mobi

ISBN-13

9781732141155

ISBN-10

1732141150

Edited by: Seth Colby and Vanya Green
Proofread by: Kathy Kandziolka and Atma Doll
Celtic Mandala by: Michael DuBois
Cover design by: Salvadore Poe
Photo of Salvadore by: Bindu Pothalil
Interior design by: Susan Gerber

Acknowledgments

I want to thank Seth Colby and Vanya Green for their excellent
work in transcribing, compiling and editing this book,
Erica Mulford and Hagar William-Olsson
for additional transcribing,
Kathy Kandziolka and Atma Doll for
proofreading the manuscript.

This book is dedicated to our beloved Lions
Den friend, Friedrich Roelli, who suggested the
idea of a "coffee table" book of Holidays.

CONTENTS

EDITORS' FOREWORD

DURING THE SUMMER OF 2019, we started the work of transcribing and editing Sal's talks for this book. We had previously worked together as a team editing some of Sal's other materials and we really enjoyed the process of working together in truth. So, we were drawn to this project as we could continue to practice the adage, when two or more meet in my name, there I will be.

If you are familiar with this work, you know that Holidays are the foundation. Our intention in working on this book was to support others to see the doubtless truth for themselves and to become their own authority. To that end, we recognize that all the words in this book are merely pointers for you to know who you really are—they are not truth. You are truth.

We did not spend any time thinking about or planning how this book would be created. Rather, the process emerged naturally and effortlessly, and we found ourselves working together joyfully whenever we felt like it. We would alternate reading each stanza aloud, slowly, pausing to recognize for ourselves if what was being pointed to was true. As we continued looking over and over again, the obviousness of the recognition became unquestioned. If we felt there was a need for more clarity in the ordering or wording, we didn't push and try to edit with "the mind," we rested in silence until the suggestions became apparent.

Sal frequently references the Bible quote, ". . . know the truth, and the truth will set you free," to reinforce the reality that there is no guru, no teacher and no expert outside of yourself. It is our hope that by reading this book slowly, taking the time you need to recognize for yourself, you will know without a shadow of a doubt that you are already, and always have been, home and the needless suffering and incessant seeking can end.

Peace,

Seth and Vanya, May, 2020

PREFACE

MY FIRST BOOK, *Liberation IS, The End of the Spiritual Path*, was transcribed and compiled from private inquiry sessions I did with people online from 2012 to 2015. It was edited for clarity, effectiveness and form. Its intention is for you to come to know your essential being, to know freedom and to be finished seeking. It is comprised of inquiries dedicated to this purpose. It also exposes the false ideas we have about liberation, ideas that keep us seeking, and never finding, forever. For those interested in my work, it is best to begin here.

The second book, *The Way of Freedom, Conversations with Salvadore Poe*, is transcribed and edited from talks I had with people in my weekly Lions Den group meetings and with people who attended my intensives here in India. This book, over 450 pages, answers many questions for people who have had a shift of knowing, know freedom and want to further resolve doubts. You will find answers to many of your lingering questions here. This helps to clarify and make doubtless what has been recognized in the first book.

This current book, *Blown Wide Open, a Collection of Holidays*, was transcribed mostly from my extemporaneous opening talks on bi-monthly online open meetings. The Holidays were never planned, or thought about in advance. As each meeting began, the words came. They have been edited for clarity, brevity and the power to elicit a clear recognition of your free essential being and your natural peace.

This book is not a page turner, it needs to be savored. Each Holiday is a facet of liberation, bringing the mind to rest more and more, until it is completely doubtless in its freedom. Reading one Holiday a day is enough. Read, re-read, recognize and then come to that recognition again and again during the course of your day. There is nothing to attain, only to recognize what is already so, and enjoy.

If you feel the Holidays are in some ways repetitive, it's for good reason. For freedom to become your natural default condition, recognizing it again and again, and then living this freedom is the key. And though you will read some of the same ideas many times, each Holiday reveals another clarifying facet of the freedom that is your essential being. For the mind to become doubtless in liberation, all of these facets have to be seen, like the pieces of a puzzle, which when viewed in whole, create the entire picture, and bring your mind to rest.

Although reading the other two books first will be very helpful, this book is also for everyone. No previous experience with meditation or self-inquiry is needed for it to be effective, as long as there is an openness and genuine willingness to see what is so clearly and simply true. For someone who has never seen my work, this book will introduce you to your free essential being, even if you are not looking for it, and will be the beginning of liberating your mind. For those who have worked with me, or read my other books, it will remind you again and again what is true and help you to come to rest as freedom. For those who know a lot about "spirituality," but have little direct experience, or are very philosophically inclined, it will clear the mind of all of that knowledge-ignorance and bring you to rest in the truth of your essential being.

Truth is very simple, obvious and ordinary. But for it to be of true value, it needs to be known and then lived, ongoingly. It is not about attaining something new, but about recognizing what is true already, and living that.

I hope you enjoy these Holidays and come to know your own freedom and peace.

Sal, Tiruvannamalai, 2020

AN INTRODUCTION TO HOLIDAYS

A HOLIDAY IS BEING BLOWN WIDE OPEN, knowing who you are, being who you are. It is both the goal of freedom and the way of liberating your mind from fear, doubt, suffering, delusion and seeking. It is the goal, in that, a Holiday reveals the truth that freedom is your natural human condition, here and now. And it is the way in that, continuing to be on Holiday resolves the tendencies that cause suffering and doubt, and brings an end to seeking anything.

When a Holiday happens there is a momentary break from thoughts. Because of our spiritual teachings, we may believe that that is the purpose of a Holiday, to be in a state of thoughtless awareness. But that is not what a Holiday is. A Holiday is about knowing. Knowing who you are. It is a 180 degree turn, from knowing something, like thoughts, sensations or sensory objects, to knowing yourself as the knowing of all of that. It is the self-effulgent light that knows itself. It is pure subject with no object. It is you knowing yourself. In this knowing, many things are revealed. These Holidays will help you to come to know for yourself what is revealed, and this knowing will lead to more and more ease and peace. There is no need to try to hold on to a Holiday and attain a "state of awareness," that is not the purpose. Know what is true, and this knowing of truth shall set you free. Know who you are, freedom itself!

While you are reading, when you see the icon ✦ look away from the book and take time to recognize what you just read, in your own knowing. There is no rush. Be sure you recognize what is being pointed to. Abide in that recognition for a moment before continuing. Once that is clear, read on until the next mandala, stop and recognize again. Come to know what is true, who are you, and what is delusion, simply mind. In this, you will come to know that you are now and always have been, free. If you allow yourself to take your time in this way, each line will reveal to you your essential being of freedom and help you to be doubtless.

KNOWING, THE
OBJECTLESS SUBJECT

THIS WORK IS ABOUT coming to know for yourself what's true, coming to know who you are essentially.

Who you are essentially is freedom itself.

Recognizing who you are essentially is the beginning of this work. It's not something that happens after forty more years of seeking. The recognition happens now. Let's look.

Relax the focus of attention.
Don't attend to any object in particular
like a thought, feeling, sensation, or sound.

Every object that's appearing is fine,
nothing needs to be excluded.

Just for a moment,
allow your attention to be open and free.

For most of us, very quickly attention will focus on an object.
Quite often that object is a thought.

A thought appears and attention focuses on that thought.

Attention may also focus on other objects
like sights, sounds or sensations.

This is completely natural,
there's nothing wrong with this movement.

Just notice when it happens.

As soon as you notice that attention
has focused on an object,
once again, relax the focus of attention,
just be open knowing.

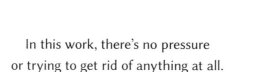

In this work, there's no pressure
or trying to get rid of anything at all.

It's about turning attention to truth.

Truth is always here and now.
It's not something you'll attain in the future.

It's what's here, now.

In truth, let's notice a few things together.

One thing we notice is that everything is included here,
all the sensory objects (sights, sounds, smells, tactile sensations)
and all the objects of thought, feeling, and emotion.

Everything is included.

When we're focused on one particular object,
which is quite often thoughts, attention is exclusively
focused on that object.

Thoughts become a world, our world in that moment.
Thoughts are apparently the only things that exist,
but it is a make-believe world.

When there's a story going on in the mind,
then that's the world that's being believed at that moment.
But, it's a world of fantasy and it's very exclusive.
Everything else is abandoned in favor of that fantasy.

Truth is abandoned for an illusory world of mind.

Let's see that function.
Just honestly see what's true,
with no judgment.

Attention focuses on thoughts
and we're in a world of thinking,
no problem.

When we notice that movement,
just stop for a moment and
be here now, open, free.

What we notice is that in truth,
there isn't only the world of illusion,
there's actually everything else as well.

Everything is included in this knowing.
Everything is known here.

The point of this and any true self-inquiry work
is to stop attending to any object,
including the thought based object called a "self."

Stop attending to any object
and instead "Know Thyself,"
which is this knowing.

A very simple way to realize this
is to know that I am.

Just see for yourself,
you can't deny it.

I know that I am.

Most of our lives when we've said, "I know that I am,"
we've meant, "I know I am this body mind organism."
We've been saying that we are an object.
However, in this investigation, when I say, "I am,"
I don't mean, "I am this body or these thoughts."

I want you to see,
I am this knowing that knows everything,
including the body and thoughts.

I am.

I can't deny, I am.

This knowing, who I am essentially, isn't an object.
It's not thoughts, sensations, or feelings.
It's not a body.

This is non-objectifiable, pure subject with no object.

I knowing I.

Within me, knowing, all objects are appearing,
including this body, thoughts, and sensations.

This is where freedom is.

Freedom is not in the future.
Freedom is not something you attain.
You recognize now that who you are is
free, no-thing.

If we're very honest, if we want to get real
and stop believing in fantasies,
which is what is required to know truth,
then we have to look now and be honest.

See, there's no past, there's no future.

In truth, there's only this,
what is.

So then, where is this ego, this self, this character
we've been believing we are for our whole life?

It's a fantasy.

If one wants to be free,
if one wants to be honest and truthful,
then look now.

There is only what is.

If you recognize this, then you recognize simplicity.
Our essential nature is the most simple thing possible.

Utter simplicity.

No-thing.

Not a single word is needed for you to know this,
not a single description, philosophy, or definition.

These words you are reading
are only intended to turn your attention to truth.

And then know, no-thing.

Utter simplicity.

Do you want simplicity?

That's what freedom is.

Words mean nothing.

All the words you've heard,
all the books you've read,
all the teachings you've listened to,

all the beautiful, poetic philosophies,
are wonderful entertainment,
but they have nothing to do with truth, none of them.

There are no descriptions needed,
names and forms are not needed.

Only knowing is needed,
which is objectless subject,
no-thing.

This is who I am, you see?

With all the apparent differences among
all the people in the world,
we can all know one thing,

I am knowing.

There is only one—I am knowing.
It's exactly the same for everyone.

Don't go to sleep in myths,
stories, and fantasies of becoming.

Wake up!

A HOLIDAY IS ABOUT
KNOWING WHO YOU ARE

Just for a moment,
look and see what's true, now.

Don't attend to any objects.
By objects, I mean those appearing through
the five senses, and any thoughts or sensations.

Don't attend to anything in particular.
Instead, just allow attention to be blown wide open.

Very quickly thoughts may appear,
and attention will focus on those thoughts.

See that movement.

Attention focuses on a stream of thoughts.
And after a few seconds, you may realize that
attention was focused on thoughts.

When you realize that, have a Holiday.

Very naturally, allow attention to be open.

A Holiday isn't about having no thoughts.
A Holiday isn't about being at peace.

A Holiday is about knowing who you are.

That's all a Holiday is,
knowing who you are.

It doesn't take time to know who you are.
In less than a second, you know who you are.

On Holiday, in open knowing,
you can say, "I am," can't you?

I am.

You don't have to say the words,
but you know you are.

I know I am.

I don't mean as a thing like a body,
a mind, or a character named [your name],
but simply, I am.

I exist.

If you say, "I am this" or "I am that,"
then you're adding something on to the end of I am—
I am this body, I am these thoughts, or I am [your name].

So, leave off the additions.
Stop at "I am."

Existing.

No-thing.

Within this no-thing, everything is appearing, isn't it?
All of the objects in your surrounding environment
are appearing and they are all appearing equally.

The body is appearing.
The furniture is appearing.

The words on this page are appearing.
The sounds are appearing.

All objects are appearing.

It's all appearing here equally, isn't it?
It's here, within this knowing.

When sensations appear in the body,
they are appearing within this knowing,
just like all the other objects you see and hear.

When thoughts appear in the mind,
they are appearing within this knowing,
just like all the other objects you see and hear.

This knowing includes everything.
Everything is included equally.

All things are equal.
They are equally known.

This is true equality.

Instead of attending to the objects that are appearing,
we're turning attention around and tending to knowing or "I."
In other words, I attending to I.

I am, and I know I am.

Let's be honest for a moment,
just be honest, look now and see.

Is there a past?
Is there a future?

Look.

Show me.

What's actually true?
What actually is?

A past?
A future?

What actually exists?

If there's no past, what happens to all
those stories you've been telling yourself?
They vanish, they're gone.

They never existed.

The truth is you are here, now, and you have no history.
If you want truth, if you want freedom,
then see for yourself,
you have no history.

Almost all of your suffering comes from
believing a history that isn't even true.

Suffering also comes from future fear, worry, anticipation,
longing, desire, and hope which isn't true either.

The only thing that can be true is what actually exists.
If it doesn't exist, then it's not true.

What's true is existence . . .

You.

Existence is you.
You are existence itself.

There's nothing behind the curtain.

There's nothing behind it, and
there's nothing in front of it.

There's only this, now.

THE WAY OF FREEDOM
IS TO BE FREE

Let's relax the focus of attention and be here now,
blown wide open.

When attention goes to anything,
which is quite often thoughts, no problem.

When you notice attention is on thoughts,
again just be open—openly knowing.

See that everything is included here,
not just the objects you are normally fixated on,
like thoughts, sensations or whatever.

Everything knowable is included here in this knowing.

Just be that.

Blown wide open, knowing.

Freedom is not difficult to recognize,
it's very simple.

As you read, be openly knowing, here.

Don't try to understand or figure something out,
just read the words and be openly knowing.

See that words appear and comprehension appears, effortlessly.
See that all the objects around you are here as well,
all the sights, sounds and sensations.

See that everything is appearing, now.

We have many ideas and beliefs about the holy grail of freedom:
It is something that is unattainable;
It is impossible to recognize;
Only one in a billion has even the slightest chance.

But the truth is, it's already your essential nature, now.

Just keep being open knowing.

What happens is, we go in the wrong direction trying to attain something called freedom. That wrong direction is called seeking, and looks like—reading books, attending workshops, watching endless YouTube videos, listening to beautiful poetic, philosophical speakers, who orate eloquently about enlightenment.

We think that if we keep listening to all these complexities and concepts, one day we'll understand it or something will happen. In the meantime, we feel that we have to listen more and more to teachers, and watch more and more videos. This is going in the wrong direction.

As you are reading these words,
as these words are appearing to you,
recognize that here and now, you are already free.

Just keep being here now, open knowing, nothing.

See, you are free.

There's no past and there's no future.

Whatever your name is,
the story of [your name] is not true,
there is no [your name].

There's only a label placed on an appearance
with a conceptual time based story attached,
none of which is true.
In truth, there is no [your name] here.

Look, now.

There's only here and now, knowing.

Keep knowing this, even as the words continue
to appear on the page.

The wrong direction is into more and more complexity of
concepts, more and more poetic, beautiful and philosophical
descriptions of enlightenment. When we listen to people who
speak beautifully, very beautifully, about enlightenment, we
don't wake up, we fall asleep.

Because freedom is so, so, so simple, the direction of pointing
should be equally simple.

Here and now,
no past,
no future,

no [your name],
nothing.

Freedom.

So then, why does it seem to be a challenge? Why does it seem to be difficult? Why does it seem to be unattainable? Because we come to know and live freedom only when we're ready, which means we're fed up with seeking, we're fed up with trying to figure life out with the mind and we're fed up with the suffering caused by believing the ignorance of the mind.

We recognize that all the books, videos, movies and concepts are a never-ending rabbit hole. We recognize that all the complexities and concepts have gotten us nowhere. Why? Because freedom isn't in that direction. It's nothing conceptual. Freedom is just being yourself, as you are, now.

Another reason why coming to freedom can seem challenging is that there are life-long samskaras and vasanas (habits, tendencies and impressions) that compel us. They can be trauma or stubbornly held beliefs we are falling for, including ideas

about what liberation is. Everyone reading this knows what freedom is. You know freedom because it's you.

The way to make freedom your default nature is not by going down the endless rabbit hole of more philosophies, more teachings or more books and videos. That's not the way, that's the wrong direction. The way of freedom is to be free, now, only now.

When you have done all the psychology, all the philosophies and all the spiritual teachings (the carousels of mind), and you realize they are not going to get you anywhere and you're fed up with them, then you'll be ready to be nothing, as you are. You can't force it. There's nothing you can do.

All the books in the world aren't going to make it happen. That's not how it works. If you think the next book, the next video, the next therapy, the next philosophy or the next spiritual teaching is going to do it, you are mistaken. It doesn't work that way. But you already know that. It works when you're ready to be free, then you will just be free.

Don't figure this out.
There's nothing to figure out.

Just look, now.

Here and now,
there's no past, there's no future,
there's no [your name],
there's no one.

There's only this, what is.

Nothing behind the curtain of now,
no meaning,
no purpose.

All of that is mind.
Meaning, purpose, time are all concepts.

Freedom is truth.
And what is truth?

No-thing,
here and now.

Be no-thing for a moment.

If you are reading this, you are ready for this message.

And then what does it take? The way of freedom is to be free—
to live this that you've come to know. And what does it look
like? On a Holiday now, when something compelling appears,
which it will, you are not interested. You are no longer fooled by
what culture and society tell you—that you have to pay attention
to the mind, thoughts and stories. Culture tells you that you
are your story—all the regrets, remorse, guilt, anger, blame,
acrimony, poor me and great me stories—it's who you are, it's
very important and you have to value it. I say that's not who
you are and has no value.

If you want to be free, you have to stop seeking, and start being
free. Yes, you will take your lumps along the way and get into
your stories, dramas, misidentifications or whatever you want

to call it. However, just keep being free and keep recognizing freedom. Just abide as freedom.

I don't mean abide now, once and forever. I mean keep coming back to freedom. Keep knowing freedom and the things that compel you will, over time, lose their power because you are no longer interested.

What are you interested in? Freedom. Nothing. Why? Because you realize that you have been a victim of a ghost your whole life. Where is the self/ego, now? Where are the stories? Where are they, now? They don't exist.

We have been victimized by all the data placed in the mind that has nothing at all to do with who we are. We didn't create and had nothing to do with any of it, yet we believe it's who we are. That's being a sheep. Someone who wants to be free no longer has the right to be a victim. You have to be a lion and just want freedom.

You just continually come to know this moment now,
which is nothing.

No past, no future.

There is no [your name], there is no story of [your name],
there is no past [your name], there is no future [your name].

That is a myth.

Do you want to be a victim to an illusion or
do you want to be free?

Reading the next book,
watching another YouTube video or
listening to the next spiritual teaching
is going in the wrong direction.

You think you're still going to get
enlightenment or attain freedom.

You aren't going to attain freedom, you already are that.

You've always been that,
you can only, always, ever be that.

You can hear this message and it can ring bells and resonate, or not. If it rings bells and resonates, you will just abide as freedom and stop being a victim. You can't choose it, but if you're ready to hear this message, that's what will happen. And there's nothing you can do about it.

All the books, videos and spiritual teachings, they're just a crutch. They're worse than a crutch, they keep you paralyzed. They keep you paralyzed!

Freedom is simple, simple, simple, simple, simple—nothing.

Be free.

I AM FULL STOP

Don't refer to body or mind,
instead know yourself,
here and now, as

I AM.

Can you say you are:

Male or female?
Black, white, red or yellow?
America, European, African or Indian?
Conservative or liberal?
Good or bad?

Remember,
do not refer to the body or mind
(just simply ignore them).
If you say you are any of those things,
you are referring to this body mind.
Ignore all of that.

If you are very truthful,
you can only say about yourself—
I am no-thing, no-definition,

I AM—AWARE, KNOWING.

Anything added on to that must be
thoughts, sensations, memories, or feelings.

So, don't refer to any of those objects for a moment,
and see, here and now,

I AM.

FULL STOP!

BEING KNOWING PEACE

LET'S MEET EACH OTHER where we are all the same, where there are no differences. Let's not meet at the level of mind—opinions, work, political affiliations, nationalities, gender or race. Let's meet where none of that applies.

For a moment, just forget anything you
believe you know about yourself.

Leave all of that behind.

Don't attend to thoughts, sensations, sights or sounds,
just allow attention to be blown wide open and free.

There is no problem with whatever comes and goes,
thoughts, sensations or anything else.
There is nothing wrong with any of it,
just don't attend to it for a moment.

Instead, simply know you are here.

This knowing is free of time.

And being free of time, what is true?

I am here, now, knowing—

nothing more.

All of our differences are in the realm of concept only.

This is very obvious.

Free of self-reference
this knowing is the same for me as it is for you.

All of your fears and anxieties
are in the realm of thought.

If you don't attend to those now,
if you leave all that behind and
be here openly knowing,
you see that who you are essentially

is peace.

In Indian philosophy, this is called Satchitananda.

Sat is existence or being.

You can't deny that you exist.
So, you can say, existence is.

I exist.

This is Sat.

The knowing of existence is called Chit.

You, knowing, know that you exist,
not as a body mind with a name and a past, but simply I am.

I know I am.

Let's just be this for a moment, so that it is clear.

I know that I exist.

Sat Chit

This is the key to freedom.

I am, and I know that I am.

Sat Chit

This, I am, and I know that I am,
has nothing to do with thought,
it has nothing to do with anything in the mind—

your past
your future
your stories
your traumas
your loves
your nostalgias
your regrets
your remorses.

It also has nothing to do with the sensations of the body.

I know that I am is free of thought and
it is free of sensation.

It's pure subject, with no object.
Simply knowing.

Recognize this.

Be this knowing that knows itself—

Sat Chit

The way to be free is to be this knowing that knows itself.

In this, you see that you are free now.

This knowing is the self-effulgent light
that knows itself.

|—|

In this I—I,
in the light that knows itself,
in this you, who knows yourself,
all of the stories of mind are gone, now.

All stresses and anxieties, fears and desires
happen in the body mind.

In your essential being,
there is none of it.

This is peace.

Your essential being is peace—Ananda.

Sat Chit Ananda—

existence, knowing itself as peace.

I, knowing myself as peace.

This is not something to do,

it is to be.

The way of freedom is to be who you are.

When we don't refer to a story of self as who we are,
and instead, consciously know ourselves as I—I,

here and now,

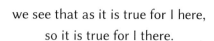

we see that as it is true for I here,
so it is true for I there.

This is where we meet properly.

So, just for a moment
be who you are.

Sat Chit Ananda.

Being, knowing peace.

NOW EXISTS—
YOU EXIST

Be on Holiday.

Thoughts may come quickly,
in a second or two, no problem.

Maybe, for a moment,
attention goes to those thoughts
and you'll be attending to the thoughts.

As soon as you notice that attention is on thoughts,
in the noticing itself, attention relaxes from the thoughts,
and attention is now open and free, for a moment.

If attention goes to a sound, sensation
or thought, it's not a problem.

Sounds are not a problem.
Sensations are not a problem.
Thoughts are not a problem.

Just notice and allow attention to be open and free.

Here, attention is open and free.

Aware is.

Just very ordinary, everyday aware.
No big deal, aware.

You can't deny it.

I'm not saying that you are doing aware.
There is no "you" to do aware.

There is just aware.

And you are that.

Within aware, everything is appearing here, isn't it?

All of the objects in the room,
all of the sounds,
all of the physical sensations,
all of the thoughts and
all of the smells.

Everything is included.
Aware includes everything equally.

What is not here is the past or the future, are they?

There is no past and future.

We are just being honest,
that's all.

That's all self-inquiry is,
just being honest.

There's no past, there's no future.
What exists is this, now.

What is this?
Who knows.
And yet, this exists.

This.

You exist.

Not as some idea of who you are:
a name, a body, all of the
past memories and traumas, and all of
the future hopes and aspirations.

This "self" story you have believed yourself
to be, doesn't exist.

That's a myth, an illusion,
an ephemeral movie on a screen.

There's no substance to it.
There is no existence to that.

There is existence to You.

You exist.

WHAT A HOLIDAY IS

Remember, a Holiday is being blown wide open knowing.

Consciously knowing that you exist.

See that now.

And consciously knowing that your existence is:

Free of time.
Free of the stories of mind.
Free of psychology, philosophy and spirituality.
Free of culture, politics and religion.
Free of the myth of self/ego.
Free of seeking.
Free of becoming.
Free of doubt.

It is
ease of being.

It is
peace.

Who you are essentially is not the body mind.

Who you are is:

Being Knowing Peace.

Look for yourself, now.

The point of a Holiday is to *know that*.
And the point of repeated Holidays is
to make that knowing doubtless.

So that, no matter if
the ocean of your being is still,
or there are ripples on the surface of you,
or there are huge waves on the surface of you,
you *know* you are free.

Waves come, of course,
small, huge, hot, cold,
pleasant, unpleasant and neutral.

That is the nature of ocean,
the nature of life, isn't it?

Why argue?

The secret is,
they all come and they all go.

And yet,
You remain.

So then, who are you?

Clearly, you are the knowing of it all—

existence, consciously knowing itself as peace with
all the ripples appearing on its surface.

Now,
it is quite natural that by having more and more Holidays
it will become more and more your default condition,
and in that, you will find yourself naturally

abiding as yourself,
Being Knowing Peace,
while walking,
while talking,
while eating,
while doing anything.

And if so,
enjoy the eternal sunshine of your natural human condition!

IN TRUTH, LIFE GETS VERY SIMPLE

THERE'S NOTHING TO THINK ABOUT with what I share.
It's the end of figuring life out, and it's the beginning of living
simple and free. Let's see.

Relax the focus of attention.
Don't allow attention to focus on anything in particular.
Instead, allow attention to be open and free,
just for a moment.

It's very natural for attention to focus on something,
like a thought, feeling or sound.

It's a natural function.

When attention is
focused on one thing in particular,
like a thought, it's mostly exclusive, isn't it?

If it's an intensely compelling thought stream,
then attention becomes quite exclusive.
We may not even be aware of anything

other than that one thought stream.
For the purpose of what we're doing here,
which is coming to know who you are essentially,
free from thoughts and emotions,
allow attention to be open and not focused on anything in particular,
and see that everything is included here, equally.

All of the sensory objects:
sights, sounds, smells, tastes, touch, sensations, thoughts, emotions,
everything is here, equally, without condition, now.

One facet known in a Holiday is
that everything is included here equally, now.

Just be openly knowing, now.

This is your natural, free condition.

Our "normal" condition is to be focused on
thoughts, fears, desires, past, future, etc.,
focused mostly to the exclusion of everything else.

Your natural condition is open and free.

When we have a Holiday,
we come to know some simple things.

For one thing, it is now, isn't it?

This knowing is now.

Obviously, knowing is now, it can only be now.
Knowing can't be any other place but now.

If you are honest,
you have to admit what's true.
Look and see what's actually true.

Don't think about it. Look and see.

Is there a past?

If you say there is a past,
it means you're looking in the mind,
you are referring to thoughts.

I'm not asking if there are thoughts about a past,
I'm asking, is there actually a past?

Likewise, is there a future?

If you say there is a future,
again that means you're looking in the mind,
you are referring to thoughts.

I'm not asking if there are thoughts about a future,
I'm asking, is there actually a future?

If you are willing to be honest, then admit,
there's no past and there's no future.

There's only what is now.

Coming to know freedom
is only about being honest, without sentiment, and
admitting what is actually true.

If you want freedom, you have to get real.

Most people don't want to get real.
They want the story of their past and future,
the myths and fantasies of
the so-called self-character.

Most people don't want to give that up.

But if you want freedom,
see for yourself what is actually true.

Don't believe me.

Is there a past?

Is it here, now?

Show it to me.

Since there's no past,
what happens to your story?
The "great you" story, the "poor you" story,
the reminiscent you, the blaming you?

All of that is a myth.
Isn't it?

If you want to be free, get real.

If you don't want to be free,
you can hang on to those stories,
play that game and die one day
still holding on to them.

But if you want to be free,
you admit that the stories are a lie,
you don't need them any longer
because you're an adult, you are free.

Look, is there a future?

Is it here, now?

Show it to me.

You have to realize that the story of your future is also a lie.

What future?

You are not going to get enlightened in the future.
You are not going to eventually understand everything.
You are not going to achieve purification,
with all your vasanas (tendencies) resolved.
Liberation is not attained in the future.

That is a fantasy.

We think that in the future,
there are things we will understand
and then we will be free.

We think we are going to understand the meaning of life,
or get answers to the questions:

Why am I here?
Where did I come from?
What is the purpose of life?
What happens when I die?

Freedom has nothing to do with understanding.
Freedom is the end of all that,
past and future, and figuring it all out.

Let's look, now.

Be no-thing.
No past, no future, just simply now.

What is the meaning of this moment?

What is the purpose of this moment?

Where did this moment come from?

Where is this moment going?

What about this moment needs to be understood?

The mind can't understand or touch life.
Life has nothing to do with the mind.

Mind is only thoughts and
thoughts are not life.

What's the way of freedom?

Being no-thing.

The way is being no-thing.

Simply alive, here and now.

In being no-thing, you see,
there's no meaning to this moment.
There's only this, what is.
What is, simply is.

Only a mind based on fear and desire
needs to know the meaning of something.

The truth of the matter is, this moment
has no meaning.

Life gets very simple
when you come to know truth,
very, very simple.

Life is ordinary and very simple.

Recognize what's true now and be finished seeking it.

Be free.
Be an adult.
Be mature.
Be simple.
Be no-thing.

Be life itself.

Stop being mind.
That's not life.

Mind makes things very complicated
and philosophical and spiritual.

This is not life, it is death.
All that knowledge and philosophy
is not wisdom, it's ignorance.

Wisdom is to have nothing,
to know nothing and
to be no-thing.

Because that is what you actually are.

Be free.
Be life itself.

Alive.

Life.

Living moment to moment,
simply.

That's intelligence.

That's wisdom.

It's the full flowering of a human being.

JUMP

When abiding as essential being you are jumped,
in mid-air, free falling.

Jump is:
when anxiety happens,
know your essential being,
free from anxiety.

Jump is:
know you are free,
once and for all.

Jump is:

the blank, white space below . . .

All questions are gone.

YOU HAVE NO HISTORY

LET'S BE HERE TOGETHER, as no-thing. Together doesn't mean together as one thing here and a separate thing there. Let's look.

For a moment, relax the focus of attention,
allow attention to be open.
When we allow attention to be open,
we notice that what is, is aware.

Aware is here.

There are a couple of non-objectifiable words
that come to mind in this recognition,

Here,

Now.

Here and now, you can say, I am.

I am, here and now.

When we say I,
we're almost always referring to this body mind organism
and our whole story of past and future,
this appearance, this time-based character.

The true I,
the only actual I,
is simply this, here and now.

Leave all of the story behind
and simply be here now as I.

Culture has taught us to believe that
who we are is this story of [your name]—
this is who I am, this story of "me,"
the past story of me and the future story of me.
We've been telling ourselves
we are this body because there are feelings here.
These feelings supposedly prove that we are the body.

We've been telling ourselves this story
our whole lives and have taken it for granted.

Let's find out who we are a little differently than that.

Simply know,
I am here.

Not as anything in particular,
as no-thing.

Don't be fooled by the feelings here.
Of course, there are feelings here.
Don't be fooled to believe that's who you are.

You are the one knowing those feelings.

Get real.

Know I.

When you know I in this way,
you can see that you are not trapped in this little body.

I is knowing.

Knowing is I.

Knowing engulfs everything.
Knowing encompasses everything.
Knowing permeates everything.

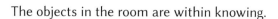

The objects in the room are within knowing.

Knowing is not trapped inside of a body.
That's just what you've been led to believe,
but what can you actually see for yourself to be true?

This work is only about coming to know
what's true for yourself, through self-inquiry.

If you see for yourself what's true,
you see that knowing encompasses everything.

The body is within knowing.
All the objects in the room are within knowing.
All the objects you see in the sky; the sun, the moon
the stars and galaxies are within knowing.

Knowing is I.

This knowing doesn't have an inside, an outside or stop somewhere.

You've been telling yourself that you are limited,
but let's look and see if it's true.
Knowing permeates everywhere.

Look!

Disregard the story of self that you believe is I,
your past history,
your future hopes,
your particular aches and pains, etc.

Know who I actually am,
which is no-thing.

If you want freedom, it's not going to happen in the future.
No one's going to get free in the future.
You don't attain freedom in the future.

You recognize freedom now.

The ideas, "I'm gonna get free in the future," and
"I'm gonna get enlightened at some point,"
are bondage, obviously.

You know what's true and truth sets you free.

You may think,
"It can't possibly be this simple.
How can this nothing be it?
How can it be?"

"There are so many teachers to listen to,
so many books (stacks of them, billions of pages)
that I have to read before I can,
maybe, attain freedom."

So then, the question is, am I ready to be free?
It's a question of seeing what's true,
without judgment.

Recognize this,
here and now,
this no-thing which has
no name,
no form,
no history.

Freedom has no history.
You have no history.

Look, now.

You, truth, have no history.
You, truth, have no future.
You, truth, have no stories.

If you want to really get real,
you have no traumas.

You have nothing.

When you recognize freedom,
being nothing, here and now, peace,
is this what you want?

Is this nothing enough?

This freedom is the end of your world,
the world of "you," the myth.

This freedom is the end of the myth of "you."
It's the end of the spiritual path.

Freedom is the end of attaining anything in the future.

Freedom is recognizing freedom now,

right now,

right now,

right now.

ABIDING IN NO TIME

You do not exist in time.
You exist now,

Blown Wide Open.

Believing in time, is believing in self.

Knowing there is no time,
is knowing who you are, free of self.

Abiding in no time,
is abiding as your essential being.

It is being who you are—
blown wide open knowing.

What do you want?
A myth?
Or truth, freedom, peace?

Who cares if there were so-called events in a so-called past?
Where are they now?

They are not, clearly!

So, why admit them into now?
Why let them disturb the peace of now?
The peace of your essential being.

The one who cares about past and future,
with all of its myths, is self/ego,
a thought, a non-existent "me."

The only you—Knowing—
has no interest in, need for
or places any meaning on
any of those myths.

That one, is the only existence.

The only reality.

Blown Wide Open

Know who you are,
in no time, now.
Be who you are, now.

PEACE IS WHO YOU ARE

Relax the focus of attention.

When attention is open and free, we notice, aware is.
Aware, very ordinary, every day, no-big-deal—aware.

You can't deny it.

I'm not saying, "There is someone who is aware,"
and I'm not saying, "Awareness is."

It's just very simple—aware.

Within aware, everything is here, isn't it?

All the objects in the room,
all the sounds,
all the smells,
all the physical sensations
and all the thoughts.

Everything is included.
Aware includes everything, equally.

What's not here is the past or the future.
Those are not included.

Look.

We're just being honest, that's all.
That's all self inquiry is, just being honest.

There is no past.
There is no future.

What exists is this—this.

What is this?

Who knows.

And what exists is You.

You exist, not as who you think you are—
a person with a name, a past and a future.

This self-story,
who you've believed yourself to be your whole life,
doesn't exist.

The past "me" story is a myth and
the future "me" story is a fantasy.

There is no substance to it, no existence.
It's just like an image on a movie screen
or a wave passing in the ocean.

There *is* existence for you.

You exist.

Leave this body, thoughts, feelings,
and everything behind for a moment.
Just ignore and "Know Thyself."

Being, Knowing itself as Peace.

Peace is known in the absence of time
and in the absence of the story of me.

Peace is the absence of time-based suffering.

What exists, what is true?

YOU!

You = Peace.

THE STORY OF
YOU ENDS

Relax the focus of attention,
don't attend to any object in particular.

Allow attention to be open,
wide open.

When attention is open and
not focused on any objects in particular,
time stops and your story stops.

The story of you ends.

You are no longer a banker, a guitarist,
a teacher, a scientist, etc.
You are none of that.

You are no-thing.

So, for a moment,
be open, no-thing, here.

See that time stops.

See that the world of self stops.

When attention is wide open,
everything is included, here and now.

Be here, now—
knowing.

Not knowing anything in particular,
just be knowing itself.

See that here, there is no story of you.
You are not anything.

What is your profession?
What is your political affiliation?
What is your nationality?
What is your color?
What is your gender?

What is your name?

Look.

You are none of those things, are you?

One thing you could call yourself is,
here and now.

You are not in the here and now,
you are here and now.

You are this!

Be openly knowing,
here and now,
who I am.

Can you stand this,
to be nothing at all,
just for a moment?

Does the mind want to grab on to the
so-called past and say, "This is me,
all these stories and traumas, etc.
are me, me, me. . . . it's who I am!"?

Does the mind want to grab on to the
so-called future and say, "I am what I imagine I'll be,
soon I'll be enlightened!"?

Does the mind want to grab on to the
sensations that are arising now and say,
"Here I am, I am these feelings!"?

Does the mind want to grab on to the
thoughts that are arising now and say,
"Here I am, I am the one thinking these thoughts, I am the
the one that is getting it, I am the one who is aware!"?

Can you stand to be nothing?

What's true is this.

This now, this is true.

What happened in the past is not true,
it's not actual.

Just be true.

Be truly who you are,
just now,
now only.

If you recognize, you see
there's no past here, there's no story.

The story is just some thoughts,
it doesn't exist in truth.

The story of a person here
that came from some place,
went through many experiences,
knows this and that,
doesn't have any truth, does it?

It's only a myth.

Whereas, what's actual,
is nothing.

This open knowing,
that has no past, no future, no self, no story,
that is nothing, is the same for me as it is for you, obviously.
This is where we meet.

Meeting at the level of mind is not truly meeting,
it's just thoughts and beliefs meeting,
stories meeting stories.

When we are here together openly knowing,
we are all the same, aren't we?

Jesus said, when two or more people come together
in my name, there I'll be.

What is his name?

Here and now!

Can you see?

There's no higher,
there's no lower,
no teacher,
no student.

There is only existence knowing itself.
It's the same for all of us.

Sat Chit Ananda—
existence, knowing itself as peace.

You, knowing yourself as peace.

This is what a Holiday is.
It's being who you are.

A Holiday isn't about having
a break or a rest from something or
getting away from or escaping anything.

A Holiday is about knowing what's true
and knowing what's not true.

This now, is what's true.

The story you've been believing your whole life
is not true, is it?

Since there is no past or future,
then there's no story of you.

What there is, is nothing.

Is nothing enough, or do you want something,
like "enlightenment" in the future?
Is truth enough or do you want something,
like to be someone, to be special?

The answer is usually, "Yes, I want to be something."

But the truth of the matter is,
you are nothing, you are no-thing.

You are only here and now.

So, just be that.

Now, you can see what the sages mean when they say,
"the greatest teaching is silence."

It's your own silence.

Now, you can see what the gurus mean when they say,
"the guru is within you."

Existence knowing itself as knowing *is* the guru.

This, is that which knows everything.
This, is the god that is all knowing, the guru.

It is each one of us.

This is where the axe comes in and chops off the head.
This is where your world ends.

NOWHERE TO GO AND
NOTHING TO DO

Just know.

Knowing equals being.

Know—you are here, now.

This is a Holiday—
consciously knowing that you are, here and now.

Being on a Holiday doesn't require you to be
still and stiff with closed eyes.

On Holiday, knowing,
you can be doing anything.

There's no need to be doing something.

Just know—I am here,
no past, no future.

Knowing is present, now.

Everything happens in knowing.

While reading the words on this page,
knowing is present, knowing is here.

It doesn't matter what's coming and what's going
because knowing is always present.

Everything is coming and going,
your whole life is coming and going,
and knowing, which is your essential being,
doesn't go anywhere.

It doesn't change and it doesn't
move through something called time.

It is now.

It is you,
and within you,
all the experiences of this life are
flowing like a river.

The ever-changing aspects are
unstable, insecure and they
cause fear, anxiety and suffering.

You, that which never changes
is perfectly stable always, peace.

There is nowhere to go
and nothing to do.

Nothing to change.
Nothing to attain.
Nothing to get rid of.

Only know what's true.

The saying is,
know what's true and truth shall set you free.

Knowing is your essential being and
knowing is already free of all the appearances.

Know what's true because truth is already free.

SEEKING DOESN'T LEAD TO FREEDOM

THIS WORK IS NOT ABOUT psychology, philosophy, spirituality, enlightenment, non-duality, advaita, etc. It is about you seeing what's true for yourself. So, let's come to know what's true.

Normally, attention is focused on something,
like work, thoughts, sensations, a movie or whatever.
Attention is focused on some "thing" that is appearing,
quite often it's thoughts.

Now, let's not attend to anything in particular.
Allow attention just to be fully open.

The point of this is to come to know something.

The most important recognition, the one that reveals everything and
reveals the falseness of everything we've believed ourselves to be,
is the very simple truth that there is no time.
Look now and see for yourself.

Freedom is about being honest.

What is actually true?
What is actual?
What is real and what is not real?

Obviously, we look here, this is real.

Real means it actually is, now.
It actually is this, whatever this is.

This, what is now, is actual.

This is what is.

What is not actual now is past or future.
There is no past and there is no future.

They don't exist.

Get real and see what's actually true.

Past doesn't exist, so anything that has to do with
this concept also doesn't exist, it's not real.

Future doesn't exist, so anything that has to do with
this concept also doesn't exist, it's not real.

If you want truth, then you don't get the lies anymore.

If you want truth, then you have to see,
nothing that you believed happened, ever happened.

Truth is only what is.

Obviously, if it isn't here now, then it's not true.
If it isn't here now, it's not real.

In truth, you see, there is only this.

In truth, everything you believe about who you are is false.

All the stories,
all the traumas,
all the terrible things and the great things you did,
all the things that people did to you, etc.
are not real, they don't exist, now.

This is actually all there is.

This is not a new age thing, like be in the now.

You have no choice.
There is only this.

You can only be now, it's all there is.

So, when are you going to get enlightened?
When are you going to get liberated?
When are you going to get free?

In the future?

What future?

You don't get liberated in the future, it's not possible.

You won't get liberated in one of your future
lifetimes like some teachings say.

If you want truth and freedom, then have it.

Here it is.

If you want to be a seeker, that of course,
has to do with the future, which deals with fantasy, fear, desire,
becoming and a "me" being something other than what's true—nothing.

If you want to be a seeker, there is no end to that.

But if you want truth, if you want freedom,
then you have to start looking now and stop seeking.

Freedom is only, ever, always now.
Freedom is only, ever, always now.

You are not going to get free, you are free.

If you believe you are going to get free in the future,
that's an ego that needs something else.
It's projecting itself into a fallacy where it is
going to get something it wants that is better than what is now,
because now is inadequate, insufficient, incomplete.

That is an endless rabbit hole.

Seeking doesn't lead to freedom.

Freedom is known, now.

There's no past.
There's no future.

It's obvious.
So, be free, now.

You don't exist as what you think you are.

You are not someone from a particular place
with all of these things that happened.
That's not who you are at all.

That "someone" is just like a character in a movie, it's not true.

If you want freedom, be nothing, now.
Freedom is nothing.

It is the end of you as a story.

The you that you believe you are,
the story of you, the past and future you
is not true at all.
That you doesn't exist.

There is only this.

There is only freedom.

This = You.

If you want freedom, start recognizing who you actually are, which is no-thing—no story. You've been very devoted your whole life to the story of the ego, the illusion, the man behind the curtain that doesn't exist. You have been devoted to a story that's not true. A very serious devotee, the best!

Be devoted to yourself, who you are, not your ego, story self. Be devoted to what is true, what is actual—you, now, here.

LIVING FREEDOM

FREEDOM IS VERY SIMPLE. To recognize this is not difficult, it's the easy part. What's not easy is breaking the habitual infatuation with the story of self. That's a habit we have had our whole life, and it's why this work has never been trivial. Breaking the habit of self-belief is what makes liberation uncommon. So, it comes down to a very simple question—What do you want?

Of course, everyone reading this is going to say, "I want liberation." But if we are honest, we see that mainly, we want to remain infatuated with mind, with our personal story and with our pains and glories.

This work is just about being honest. It's about recognizing your essential nature, which is free already and seeing how the mind continually goes in the wrong direction: I don't want that; I want my beliefs, ideas, concepts; I want my fears and desires, my regrets and sentimentalities; I want my spirituality and philosophies; I want my poor me stories and my great me stories; I want my hopes of salvation in the future. There's nothing to judge, no right or wrong. It's just about being honest, just knowing what's true. By seeing and being devoted to what is true, the light of your essential being, all ignorance will burn away. By being honest, you will know what is keeping you bound. No sadhana (spiritual practice) needed. Why? Because freedom is already the case. If you want it, have it!

Let's see what's true, it's very simple. Let's start off at the beginning, which is also the end—freedom.

Just be here, blown wide open.

We can see, now,
that there's no past or future,
there's only this, what is.

What is, is.

See for yourself.

If you like telling stories,
you can start talking about some past stories of "me,"
or some future stories of "me."

It doesn't make them true.

What's actually true is this,
this moment now, here.

Stay in this knowing of now.

Notice,
I know that I am here.

I know that I am here now, knowing.

Knowing is not knowledge,
information or description,
it's just knowing that I am.

This knowing is the real knowing.

All information,
philosophy, descriptions
or thoughts of past and future
are just knowledge, not knowing.

You are the knowing
that knows all the knowledge.

Instead of attending to any objects of knowledge,
just know yourself, I.

This is what the Bible means by "Know Thyself."

Abide as I for a moment—
no words, no descriptions, nothing.

The "I" I'm speaking of is not a thing.
Even the word "I" is too much.

For a moment, get rid of the word "I."

When you first came out of the womb,
there was no "I am something."
There wasn't even the word "I."

There was only this, no-thing.

For a baby, objects are still known. They aren't known as name
and form, but they are known in the field of knowing. If an

object appears in front of a baby, the baby is cognizant of it, but not as a separate object. It just appears in the field of knowing.

Eventually, everything is named and labeled. A world is created with names, concepts, descriptions and forms. The "me" story is built on that and now, there's apparently a big story of a me here, with a big past and a big future, including all the beliefs, traumas, nostalgia, regrets, wishes, hopes and fears. But look, now.

Where is the "me" story?

It's not actual, is it?

If we simply look now, we see
that in fact, nothing has ever happened.

You are exactly as you were when you came out of the womb.

Look now and see,
don't take my word for it.

Look, now.

This has never changed,
nothing has ever happened.

All of these apparent events,
that we think happened in an apparent time,
where are any of them now?

It's very simple and obvious
for those who have the openness to hear and see.

It's not difficult.

So now, the question comes,
what do you want?

There's a lot of false information in the beliefs, concepts, nostalgia, traumas, and poor me and great me stories. And, if we are being honest, mostly we want that. We don't want to be finished with that because if we are finished with that, we think, "Who the hell am I? You mean I have to give up the whole sixty years of my life?"

In truth, you're not giving up anything because none of that actually is. However, for all our lives, we've believed so strongly that the stories are who we are that now, we believe we're giving up our ego and dying, but that's not true—it's just a fear based on an idea. Nothing is dying, nothing is being given up, except what's not true. I still am. I am still here, untouched.

Also, we think we're giving up our future hopes of enlightenment, liberation and all of our other future desires. Again, that's just an idea. If we give up all of those ideas, what do we actually lose? We don't lose anything, except the idea of a future, which is only created by our hopes and fears now. All of it is conceptual, not actual. None of it exists. We lose nothing and instead, gain the kingdom, freedom, which is already, always the case anyway. You've never not been free.

There are also cynical ideas that if you give all of that up, you are going to be nothing and life is going to be no fun. No! Life is ever-present, it's ever new, fresh and alive, now. The story of self is non-existent, it is not alive, it's death, it's dead. In freedom, you can fully enjoy life—fully alive.

Recognizing who you are takes no time at all. Of course not, it's already the case. It doesn't take any time to go from here to here. You've always been here!

The end of the spiritual path is now, it's this.
This is the end of the spiritual path.

There is no path from here to here.
There is no book that can get you here.
There is no practice that can get you here.

No sadhanas will get you here.

You are here!

No books are needed.
My books are tools to point to this,
then throw the books out.

No words are needed.
The words you are reading now are tools to point to this,
then throw the words out.

There is just knowing, now.

This takes no time,
no practice.

It's the end of seeking.
It's the end of the spiritual path.

This already is the end,
it's already liberation,
it's already freedom.

Know truth and be devoted to truth.
Be devoted to truth instead of
being devoted to the lies of self.

When regret, nostalgia or fear of the future come up,
once again, know what's true and be free, now.

Be free, be free, be free—

live freedom, now and forever.

FRUIT FROM THE TREE
OF KNOWLEDGE

THE BITE OF THE FRUIT from the tree of knowledge is the bite that says, "I am separate . . . me." Until that bite happens, there is nothing separate because there is no me to be separate from anything else.

And that bite didn't just happen once when you were a baby and you finally believed your mother that you were separate and your name was [your name]. That's the first time it happened, but it has happened a million times since then.

Every moment you refer to yourself as me, you bite again of the fruit from the tree of knowledge. You go from being fully open, aware, no-thing, no self, no ego, to a very limited exclusive focus—I am separate. In this, your world of me is created and with it all the world of separation.

This is Original Sin.

It is a reflexive habit. We don't know we are doing it and it is without volition. Yet, it's pretty constant—me, me, me . . . There are breaks, but they are very brief, maybe a second or two.

Holidays are a way for you to come to know your essential nature—knowing.

> In a relaxed way,
> without any force or effort,

allow attention to be open.
Just be open.

For a vast majority of our lives,
we are habitually attending to objects.

The normal human condition
is to be focusing on something—
thoughts, sensations or feelings.

Now, for a moment,
don't focus on anything in particular.

Be here,
open knowing.

When you came out of the womb,
before all of the data was put in your brain,

which distracts you and keeps you
focused on me, me, me,
your condition was this.
Fully open, all-inclusive.

Come to know yourself as this—
fully blown wide open
with no center at all.

Be here, knowing.

Knowing what?

Simply knowing yourself as knowing.

Attend to this,
just being here open, knowing.

Knowingly open, that's all.

As you are reading this, you may realize you are having a recognition or you may not realize you are having a recognition and think, this isn't anything special. There are a range of different experiences this recognition elicits.

To be clear, a Holiday is not about having no thoughts, it is not about being at peace, it is not about being spacious. A Holiday is about shifting from believing you are this body mind organism to knowing who you are. A Holiday is about knowing who you are.

And in that knowing, your entire life is completely demolished, immediately. You see that it's false. Everything you've believed you are or have been is over.

AWARE

Just now,
in this moment,
be aware,
just aware itself.

It is very simple,
so simple you may not notice.

Aware is your nature.

So, just be AWARE,
and you will then see that all objects,
including the object, a felt sense of I am here in a body,
arise in you—

AWARE.

AWARE, a bird singing.

AWARE, a stomach ache.

AWARE, a thought attack.

AWARE, a seeker.

AWARE, the words on this page.

AWARE, an emotional upset.

AWARE, the feeling of anger in your gut.

AWARE, bliss.

AWARE, ecstasy.

AWARE, agony.

AWARE, the greatest mystical experience you have ever had.

AWARE.

Who you are.

I AM THAT I AM

WHAT WE'VE BEEN TAUGHT and trained to do, and all we've known to do our whole life, is to attend exclusively to objects. We put all of our value and emphasis on objects as if they're the most important thing. Of course, we believe the most important object is me—I, this self.

My thoughts, my feelings, my beliefs, my stories, my sensations, my past, my future are the most important objects. This "me" story is the object we worship. We are very devoted to it.

What we don't do, and what we're going to do together now, is leave that story behind.

Don't attend to that story at all.
Instead, just be here now, knowing.

Knowing.

Knowing is not exclusive,
it includes everything.

Everything is included and
everything is equal.

All objects are equal in that
they're all known.

Whether it's the objects in your room, the sounds you hear,
the feelings in the body, the thoughts in the mind or
the words on this page, they are all equally known.

Also, all objects are equal
in that they are all transient.

Everything comes and everything goes,
there is no exception.

Sights come and go.
Sounds come and go.
Sensations come and go.
Thoughts come and go.
Emotions come and go.

Nothing remains permanently in the realm of appearance.

All appearances are equal,
they are all known and
they are all transient.

In being here now, simply knowing,
everything is known.

To whom? To you.

I know.

Knowing is not a thing.
It's not, I am this or I am that.
It's not, I am this body or I am this story.

It's, I am no-thing.

I simply exist.

If we honestly look now, is there a past?

Most people say,
"No, but I have some thoughts about a past."

That's not what I'm asking.
I'm not asking if there are some thoughts
that are referring to something called a past.
I'm asking what is actually true,
what is actual, what exists, what is?

Is there a past?

Look now.

Of course,
the answer is no.
There's only this, now.

Is there a future?

Again, of course, the answer is no.
There's only this, now.

What exists, what is actual,
what is true, what is real is only this,
what is appearing now.

Here and now, since there's no past,
your whole life story is a myth.

If this is true for you, then it must be true for everyone.

All of our life stories are myths,
they're only thoughts appearing now.

If all our stories of the past and future
are myths and fantasies,
what does that leave us with?
Nothing.
I am.

No story, no self, no ego.

We can all say the same thing, can't we?

I am, now.

This is true, we can't deny it.

The "I am [your name]" story is a myth.

Where is anything that supposedly ever happened?
Where is it?

Do you want to continue to be a victim of all those stories
or do you want to be free?
Most people want to continue to be a victim of their stories,
their stories of hope and fear.

If you want to be free, you have to admit what's true.
The Bible says, know what's true and truth shall set you free.

Truth is simply this.

This is true for all of us.
There is only one experience happening right now.
It's knowing, open knowing.

Knowing here is the same as knowing there.
Everyone can say, "I know that I am."

When Moses asked God his name,
God replied, "I am that I am."

You can also say, "I am that I am,"
can't you?

This is where we meet.

We meet now.

Coming to know freedom is just about being honest
and not believing myths of the past and fantasies of the future.

Freedom is about getting real.

What is real?
This!

This, here, is obviously real.
You can't deny this.

Freedom is always present,
it's the only thing that's ever present.

This is good news
as there's nowhere to go.

What I'm showing is ridiculously simple. It's too simple. It can't
be this simple, can it? Well, actually it is this simple. However,
I'm respectful because as simple as this is, it's not trivial. We
have a lifetime of vasanas (tendencies), samskaras (mental
impressions), habits, beliefs, thoughts, ideas and concepts. They
have a momentum and they keep distracting us and compelling
us into ignorance, doubt, and misidentification.

So, it's not over with one recognition of truth. One in ten million
are finished abruptly, like Ramana Maharshi, but for most of us,
that's not the case.

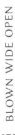

We first recognize what's true, which takes no time. Then, by staying devoted to truth, the vasanas and samskaras won't fool you any longer because they don't have the power.

The longer you stay devoted to truth, the more knowing becomes your default nature.

WHAT IS SATSANG

WHAT IS THE MEANING of the word satsang? It is not clearly understood, and is often considered to be something that someone gives (e.g. He is giving satsang). That is a misunderstanding. Satsang is not given. Satsang means being together in truth. Jesus spoke about satsang—when two or more people come together in my name, there I'll be. Being together in truth is satsang. Let's be together in truth, now.

Allow your attention to be open,
very relaxed, with no force or effort.

Just be freely open.

It's okay to scratch your nose, the back of your head or whatever.

All kinds of things are happening—
sights, sounds, smells, thoughts and sensations.
Nothing is wrong with any of it.

Instead of attending to anything in particular,
just be open, openly knowing, here.

So, what's the point of this?

It isn't to get into a state of never attending to something.
That's not the point.

The point is to come to know what's true, this.

Notice a few things.

Without attending to anything in particular,
see that everything is included, everything is appearing.

Everything is equal,
which means that everything is known, equally.

The words on this page,
the objects in your field of vision,
the sounds,
the sensations in the body,
the thoughts,
everything is equally known.

Normally, we are fixated on one particular object,
the object of "me," self.

So, just for a moment, let's not fixate on self,
or on anything in particular, and notice that everything is here,
including thoughts, sensations, sounds and sights.

Let's be here for a moment.

You can say that this,
whatever is appearing now, is true.

What you are knowing now is true.

We can debate the veracity of how true
anything is because everything is insubstantial,
but for this purpose, what's appearing now,
what is, is true because it's appearing.

What's true is what is appearing,
including all the visual objects,
all the thoughts, etc.

They're all appearing, now.

But what's not true?

Something called "the past."
That's not true, is it?

What else is not true?

Something called "the future."
That's also not true, is it?

This "self" that we are focused on so often
is the story of a past me or the story of a future me.

It's past stories—this happened to me
and that happened to me, I did this and that person did that.
It's future stories—I'm afraid of this, I'm afraid of that,
I'm going to get enlightened and I'm going to die.

All of those stories,
that's "self."

But let's have a look.

Where is any of that now?

There's no truth to any of it.

We waste most of our lives on this lie of self,
on a myth of past self and a fantasy of future self.

Just for a moment, let's not live that lie,
Let's be truth together, here and now.

Don't even focus on the sensations that are appearing.
Don't deny them, just don't attend to them.

Don't attend to anything.
Attend to knowing,
nothing.

Knowing is now.

I know.

Not,
I know anything in particular,
simply—I know.

Now, the movie of self ends.

It's a movie playing in your knowing,
this movie of past and future.

Just as a movie has no substance—
no actual people, no actual drama, no buildings on fire—
the movie of self has no substance.

The world of self—the whole world that's created
by past and future—is not actual.

This now is actual.

This.

This is the end of that world.
That world is finished, now.

The world of "you" is finished, now.

That "you" doesn't exist.

If you want freedom, you have to get real.

You have to get real, now.
You have to be honest.

Freedom is about being honest.

There are over seven billion people on the planet, each with
completely different stories, different worlds of "me"
that have no meeting point whatsoever, none.

Normally, each of us are living within our own little world of delusion.

But when we are honest
and truthful enough to just be here and now,
all of those separate worlds vanish.

And what's left is the same for everyone—
knowing, simply knowing.

In this way, we are meeting in truth, together.

It's nice to meet this way.
There're no past and no future stories anywhere.
There's no higher or lower, no better or worse.

Everyone's equal, equally knowing.

As you can see,
this recognition is very simple,
here and now,

It's very simple.

This is satsang.

FREEDOM ALREADY IS

There is only now.

What is here is aware.

Your essential nature is aware, free, all-inclusive.

Is it true?

Here and now, the only thing you can't deny,
and needs no evidence other than itself is:

I am aware, here and now.

This is self-evident,
not depending on any external object,
any thought or any feeling.

True?

If you recognize that it is true for you,
then it must be true for everyone, right?

Without projecting to tomorrow
or five minutes from now,
isn't it already doubtless, right now?

I am no-thing.

Self is a story we have come to believe
and have taken for granted.

It has to do with time.

But where is time?
There is only now.

Jump off the story of self.

See that there is no story, no self, now.

If you don't refer to a thought that self is here, where is it?
If there is no time, where is it?

So then, it is already finished, isn't it?

It's finished, now.

Just keep coming to see it is finished.
It is already doubtless, now, in this moment.

Don't go in the mind, just don't do it.

Stay jumped for a moment.
Don't attend to any thoughts or feelings that are appearing.

Keep jumping into no-thing.
Free, open, spacious aware.

No-thing.

Just for a moment, see—
now, I am free,
now, it is doubtless.

This is very simple.
It is no-thing.

It is the same for all of us.

We are all the same, essentially, aren't we?

If this is clear,
what more is there
than this, no-thing?

What is there to transcend or attain?

What philosophy is needed?
What spiritual practice?
What book?
What description?
What satsang?

If it is recognized to be true, stick with this.

If it is recognized to be true, why be the
prodigal son and go some other direction to
try to get something more—

more books,
more spiritual ideas,
more philosophies,
more mystical experiences,
more meetup groups?

If you want freedom, it is clearly here, now, isn't it?

You don't get to fulfill all your ideas about "enlightenment"
that you got from reading books or listening to teachers.

You don't get any of it.

You get no-thing,
freedom.

If it is seen that this is true, then why do anything else?

The ultimate answer to all spiritual questions is:

no questions, no answers.

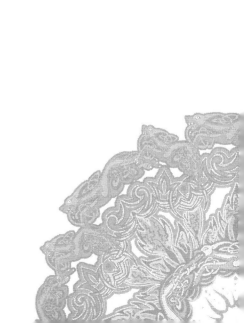

SPIRITUAL TEACHINGS: ANYTHING BUT NOTHING

Allow your attention to be completely open,
very naturally and easily.

Don't look for anything,
there's nothing to find.

Notice, here and now,
fully open, knowing.

Everything is included, isn't it?

All of the objects in your room,
the words on the page,
the sensations, the thoughts—
everything is here, it's all included.

However, some things aren't included,
like all the spiritual books you've read.
Where are they now?

All those great spiritual books, filled
with all those words and beautiful concepts,
do they have anything to do with this, now?

All those YouTube videos,
thousands of them,
look, where are they?

Do they have anything to do with this, now?

Be real and look at what actually is.
What is actually here and now?

This, here and now,
is it a concept?
Is it a spiritual insight?
Is it a great spiritual philosophy?
Look, is THIS like any of that?

What actually is,
THIS,
here and now,
is very ordinary.

It's just you, here and now, knowing.

It's not a concept.

Because of all the books we've read and
all the teachers we've heard, we have a lot of ideas,
expectations and spiritual concepts—
not one of them has anything to do with

You,
Here,
Now,
Ordinary,
Knowing.

Do they?

They have to do with concepts—
non-duality, non-separation, merging with the divine, etc.—
anything but nothing.

You see?

Anything but nothing is what all those books
and teachers have convinced you of.

This thing called non-duality is just a concept.

Look,
what is true, now?

Be here, now, nothing,
absolutely nothing,

no past,
no future,
no books,
no videos,

nothing,
empty,
naked.

YOU ARE WHAT NEVER CHANGES

For a moment, know,
know that you are here.

When you know you are here and now,
you are immediately out of the concept of
time, which creates a mythical past and future.

Knowing you are here
is the end of time.

There is no time.
It's not an actual thing.
Time is only thought, a concept.

So, just know you are here.
Just know, that's all.

Nothing to do with time,
past or future.

In the saying, know you are here,
the knowing is you.

The knowing is what never changes,
you see?

It has always been this.
You have always been knowing.

So, just be yourself for a moment.

This you, this knowing, doesn't change.
It's always been the same.

What does change, constantly,
is that which your name refers to.

And everything this name refers to,
all the identities, the stories, the traumas,
doesn't exist, does it?

But you exist, right?

Knowing.

Until we come to see something different,
we take for granted that we are a name,
a body and a story of past and future.

That's who you have been taught you are.
That's who you believe you are,
until something else is known.

Recognize that you exist only now.
You don't exist as a name, a body or as a
story—that story is a myth.

You only exist now.

You are the knowing that knows its own existence, now.

This is you.

You know it's true because it's always been the same.

Throughout the whole apparent body mind
lifestream, it's always been you, knowing.

Throughout all of the changes of this body mind,
one thing hasn't changed.

You.

TRUE MEDITATION

I'M SURE A LOT OF PEOPLE reading this meditate. I used to meditate eight hours a day for years. I thought meditation was closing the eyes and trying to get into a state of peace, bliss, no thoughts, or whatever. However, that's not really meditation. Why don't we find out what meditation is?

Relax the focus of attention.
Instead of attending to any particular objects,
like thoughts, sensations or sounds,
for a moment, just allow attention to be blown wide open.

Be relaxed, not stiff.

Maybe some thoughts will come, no problem.
When you notice attention has gone to those thoughts,
just relax the focus of attention and
allow attention to be blown wide open.

Scratch your nose, move a little bit, no problem.

There are visual objects appearing,
there are sounds happening,
there are sensations in the body,
there are thoughts coming and going,
the words on this page are appearing.

Everything is perfectly fine.

Don't attend to any of them.
Just know.

Blown wide open knowing.

Knowing is here,
not knowing something in particular,
not intellectual knowing,
not knowledge, not description.

Simply knowing, in which everything is appearing.
Know this.

Instead of attending to any particular objects,
attend to yourself—knowing.

I am and I know that I am—
simply, I am existing.

If you notice "I am existing," you notice it is now.

You don't exist within anything called a past or a future,
you exist now, simply, knowing.

See,
in this knowing,
none of your history is here at all.

Where are all the stories of your life—where you came from,
your political and religious affiliations, your traumas?

Where are any experiences you've allegedly had—mundane or spiritual,
anything you did right or wrong?

Look, here and now, blown wide open knowing.

None of that exists.

Be honest, none of it exists.

But you exist, and you can't deny it.

You can't deny, I am, here and now.

Just be honest, there is no time—
you have no history,
nothing ever happened.

Here and now, I am.

If you recognize you have no history,
then you also recognize, it is the same for everyone.

Everyone is equal in this way,
no teacher, no student, no guru, no devotee.

There are sensations, there are sounds, there are visual objects
appearing now and they are all appearing to you—knowing.

The sensations appearing are known to you
exactly as the words on this page are known to you.

The words and sensations are equal.
Both are objects, equally known to you.

The sensations, which you've been conditioned to think you are,
are known to you as an object, just like the words on this page are known to you.

In coming to know this,
you have a 180 degree shift from knowing some object,
like the words on this page or the sensations in the body,
to I knowing I, not as a thing, but as knowing.

This is the true knowing—pure subject with no object.

All thoughts, sensations, sensory objects
and experiences are changing.

Within I, knowing,
everything is changing constantly.

Be here now and look.

You are here, knowing.

Now, some words appear on the page,
and you are knowing the words.
You were here before, during and after
the appearing of these words.

Similarly, in the midst of any experience,
you are knowing the experience,
and when the experience is gone,
you are here knowing.

You are here knowing, before, during and after
every single experience that ever appears.

Every thought, every sensation, every mundane and mystical experience
and every amazingly blissful experience that ever happens,
you are here knowing, before, during and after all of it.

So, why value any experience, even bliss?

Value yourself because you're free.

You = Knowing.

Knowing = Freedom.

This is the real bliss.

The bliss that does not end.

The freedom that does not end.

You, who does not end.

In the midst of you, comes an unpleasant sensation or emotion
and you are here before, during and after that sensation or emotion,
fully blown wide open knowing.

All unpleasant experiences you've ever "had" are gone.
Look, where are they now?

They are gone, and you're here.

So why fear them?

Throughout your entire life, how many hundreds of thousands
of experiences have passed through the body mind organism?

Where are any of them, now?

The good ones and the bad ones,
where are any of them, now?

The most exalted mystical experiences,
where are any of them, now?

They are not here.

So, they are meaningless.

What is meaningful is you,
that which doesn't change.

And you find this out simply by coming to know yourself—
knowing, pure subject, no object.

I knowing I.

I am and I know that I am,
not as anything in particular, just pure knowing—I.

It's the same for me, it's the same for you,
it's the same for your most beloved guru.

Ramana, Jesus, Buddha tell you they're the same as you.

Even if you say, "No master, you're exalted and I'm lowly,"
they tell you, "You're the same as me—"
blown wide open, I knowing I, here and now.

This is meditation.

Knowing who you are is meditation.

And knowing who you are is being who you are,
it's exactly the same.

Knowing and being are the same.

Scratch your nose, move around,
dance, work, no problem.

Sitting still with eyes closed and focused concentration
on trying to get something is not true meditation.
Keep trying! You won't get it that way.

Let's meditate as we are.

These words are appearing, you see them on the page,
you comprehend them effortlessly.

They are appearing to you as are all the other objects in your environment.

You don't know what the next words will be and yet, they appear to you.

You, knowing.

This is meditation, while you are reading,
blown wide open knowing.

SEEING NOW AS
ONE EXPERIENCE

When you look at a painting,
with its blending of colors, shapes and textures,
you experience one painting.

When you listen to a symphony,
with its interwoven melodies, chords and rhythms,
you experience one symphony.

When you look at this present moment,
with its countless sights, sounds, smells, tastes and sensations,
you experience this one moment.

Just like a painting,
just like a symphony,
now is one experience.

Who knows this one constantly changing,
experiential moment, here and now?

You.

Who are you then?

Now.

What knows, and what stays the same
throughout the ever-changing experiential landscape?

I am here, now.

Clearly,
you can see that no experiential moment
has lasted or has been substantial.

In fact,
experience is in non-stop,
constant change.

You are the knowing of it all.

So then,
why place an inordinate value on that which is
ephemeral, insubstantial, here and then gone,
while completely overlooking the essential unchanging aspect of it all?

Peace is found here, now.

YOU!

WHO AM I

I am consciously aware that I exist.

This is the essential truth of who I am.

If I say, "I exist . . . as something," that
is the objective, ephemeral aspect of who I am,
only apparently true.
Who I am essentially is existence, consciously knowing itself.

My essence is formless peace.

My temporal form is all of the known objects.

As myself, I essentially,
exist peacefully,
non-changing,
eternally knowing.

As manifestation, I appear
as the constantly changing objects of perception.

All objective aspects arise,
persist and subside in my essential being.

They have no independent nature,
and as such, do not exist separate from me.

They appear as ripples on the surface of me,
as a wave appears on the surface of ocean.

They are never different from me, their source.
They are never separate/independent from me, their source.

Look.

All there is, is me.
All that is known is me.

KNOWING, YOUR ACTUAL EXPERIENCE

WE HAVE THE BELIEF that we are inside this body, here, looking out of these eyes—there's a "me" in here looking out at the world. That's just an idea, a belief, ignorance instilled in us by culture and society. It's not actually your experience. Your actual experience is expansive.

In your actual experience, the appearance called a body is just one small aspect of everything that is known, here and now. It's just an assumption that we are inside a body and it is something we have never really questioned, until now.

Relax the focus of attention, don't
attend to any one object in particular,
and just allow attention to be open and free.

Be knowing and
notice something.

You are here, knowing,
open and free.

Everything is known here:
all the objects in the room,
all the sensations and all the thoughts,
everything is known, now.

Don't know any appearance in particular,
don't deny anything,
just know the simple fact of knowing.

Each of the different appearances
have one thing in common—they are all known.

All appearances come and go.
Thoughts and sensations are always
appearing and disappearing—constantly changing.

But knowing does not change.

So, instead of attending to any particular object
that's coming and going,
just be knowing.

Your essential nature is knowing.

Knowing is not an object,
it's not a thing.

Let's look at our actual experience.

The body exhibits something called
consciousness (a felt sense of I am here)
and because of that, we assume that
knowing is limited to the body
and we are looking out of these eyes
at the rest of the world out there.

When you relax the focus of attention,
you see that you have no head
and you have a wide open view.

Knowing is not inside something.

It is not limited.

It is ubiquitous.

All the objects of perception are imbued with knowing.
Everything you see, hear, feel or sense
is imbued with the knowing of it.

Even the sun, the moon, the stars and galaxies
are not out there, they are right here in knowing.

They do not exist without the knowing of them.

Look and see.

Knowing is not limited inside a body.

Look,
is there a line where
knowing begins and ends?

See,
there is no inside/outside.
You, knowing, are not limited to a body.

Knowing is all inclusive and all encompassing.
The farthest galaxy is right here in knowing, in you.

Rest here.

It's called Sat Chit Ananda.

Sat—You exist.

Chit—Knowing.

You exist as knowing.

To know who you are,
is to be who you are.

This is Peace—Ananda.

I AM NOTHING

A HOLIDAY IS WHAT THE WORD IMPLIES. It's being on a
Holiday from everything, and I mean everything.

Just for a moment, allow attention to be open.

There's nothing wrong with any of the senses,
we're not trying to escape anything.
We're being open, aware,
not attending to anything in particular.

Attention moves freely
when it's not attending to anything in particular, and
we recognize that everything is here, isn't it?

When we attend to one thing in particular,
that becomes the locus of attention, the focal point.
Especially, an intense thought or emotion,
those can be the most compelling.

Focused attention creates an entire world,
one where there isn't space for anything else.

But when we allow attention to be open and free,
we see in fact everything is included equally, everything.

Everything here is known equally.

We also see that this knowing
is not located inside the body.
There isn't a line at the skin where
the world begins and you end.

See that knowing is ubiquitous, omnipresent.

See, it isn't stuck somewhere and
that everything is included.

Knowing includes everything that is actual, now.

See, knowing can only be now.
It's obviously only now.

What's not included in knowing are concepts
that don't exist in reality.

It doesn't include myths,
like the past and all of the stories of the past.

All of the so-called stories don't exist, they're not true.

Knowing may include thoughts about a past,
but it doesn't include any of the actual events
that the thoughts are referencing.
If a thought is telling a story, that story is not actual.
It's only a thought appearing now.

So, in truth, what's not included in knowing
is something called a past.

Why?

Because it's not true.
It's not actual.

Knowing only includes what's actual,
and that's everything that is.
The past is not and neither is the future.
The fantasy of the future is not actual,
there is no such thing.

Be open knowing, now.

See, there's no such thing as past or future,
just open knowing, now.

Truth is what is.

If it is not, then it's not true.
It's a story of some sort.

What is, is.

Only what appears now is known.
Only what appears now is true.

Whatever objects are in your room,
whatever sounds you are hearing,
whatever thoughts you are perceiving,

they are appearing now,
that's what's true/actual.

Any story of the past or future is a complete lie.

Some teachers say, "Only the real is true."
What does that mean?
It just means what is now is true,
anything else isn't true.

Let's see what else isn't true.

We've all read spiritual books.
How many spiritual books have you read?
10, 20, 30 . . . ?

So many words, philosophies and descriptions.

Look now.
Where are they?

All the books (including mine), philosophies, ideas, and
concepts we have about enlightenment, freedom, what
happened in the past and what's going to happen in the future,
where are they?

They are not true.

If we want to know what's true,
then we have to give up everything that's false.

It's very simple.

Everything that's false is what's not true, now.
And what's not true now is every single Ramana Maharshi book,
because where are those words now?

If you want to know what's true
they say, you have to kill the Buddha.

What's the Buddha?
Is it some guy?

No, the Buddha is all your stories,
spiritual concepts and books.
That's the Buddha that has to be killed.

It is the mind.

And how is it killed?

By seeing that it's not here, now.

It's not true.
There's no truth to any of it.
What's true is you.

Look.

Can you live without those books or the next YouTube video?
Can you live with nothing like that?

Being free means living free, now.
Being free isn't something that's going to happen
in the future after you read the next book.

Being free is living free now, with nothing.

Nothing.

By nothing, I mean there is no self, no character.

There is nothing.

The character you've believed yourself to be
your whole life does not exist.

It is not true, it's a lie.

If you look for that person,
that character you believe yourself to be,
and if you're honest,
then you'll see there's nothing.

Look now, where is it?

Those books, spiritual concepts and philosophies that are in the mind
are not separate from this character "you."
Those are the character, the "you" that you think you are.

When you get rid of those books, spiritual concepts and philosophies,
you see that the false "you" doesn't exist.

We've been conditioned to believe that all the spiritual concepts
appearing in the mind reference an existent character, an ego, a self.

When the concepts go, that "you" goes.

See?
There's nothing.

Even these words have to go.
I use a few words that are not objectifiable to serve as pointers.
They're just a few words to show you something,
but they have to go as well.

Like the word now,
there's nothing called the "now."
There's no "now" that's an actual *thing*.
It's just a word to point you to see what's true.

I also like to use the word knowing,
because whatever objects are appearing now are known.

Knowing is not an object,
it is not a thing,
but knowing is here, now.

Existence is another word I like to use.
You can say, "I exist," not as a *thing*, simply, I exist.

But those words have to go as well.
Throw those words out and there's nothing.

Of course, our cultures and religions have not taught us this.
Our whole lives, we've been conditioned to believe we are *something*:
special, unique, individual, the doer with free will,
a Christian, a Buddhist, American, European, Indian, etc.

So many things you supposedly are.
So I ask, can you be nothing?

If you want truth,
see what's true, *now*.

If you want truth, don't think about what's true
in the so-called future or in the so-called past.
Look now and see that there's nothing behind the curtain.

There's only nothing.

Can you have nothing—

no stories,
no hopes,
no fears,
no desire for freedom?

Nothing.

Can you know nothing—

no past,
no future,
no philosophies,
no concepts about enlightenment?

Nothing.

Can you be nothing—

not a Buddhist,
not a Non-Dualist,
not an Advaitist
not any label?

Nothing.

You have nothing,
you know nothing
and you are nothing.

Can you just be?
Period.

COME TO REST AS
WHO YOU ARE

Don't attend to any objects in particular,
any thoughts, feelings, sensations
or any objects known to the senses.

No need to deny anything,
but don't attend to anything at all.

Just be here knowing.

Attend to knowing itself.

Not knowing anything in particular,
just knowing itself.

Knowing is primary.

See that when you do this,
you come to rest.

Knowing, knowing itself.

I don't use the word awareness because
it is objectifiable, it can be considered a "thing."

You are not "something" called awareness.

Knowing is not objectifiable.

Knowing is not separate from you.

What knows all objects is knowing.
What knows knowing is knowing.

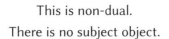

This is non-dual.
There is no subject object.

It is pure subject with no object.
It's knowing.

It's you.

You don't have to meditate
for another thirty years
or read seven hundred more books
to find out who you are.

Look, now.

Know—I am, knowing.

Of course, it's so simple.
It's too simple.

We think it has to be more
because it says so in the books.

In truth,
you know that you are now.
You know that you exist now, as knowing.

So, come to rest as who you are.
Be who you are—knowing.

Knowing is the same as being.
Being = Knowing.

To Know Thyself is to Be Thyself.

See that this knowing, who I am,
here and now, is the end of your whole world.
It's the end of the whole story
you have been believing yourself
to be for your whole life.

Look, now.

Where are all the stories, beliefs, ideas,
opinions, attitudes, impressions,
the whole character of self?

Does any of that exist, here and now?

Where?

That whole character of you is just thought.

It's not true.

NOTHING MORE TO SEEK

Relax the focus of attention.

On Holiday, you can be doing anything,
reading the words on this page, walking, eating, talking, etc.
You don't have to be sitting in a stiff meditation posture.

You are just open knowing.
Open, free, knowing, here and now.

There is no past, no future, no story of me.
None of that is actual.

What is here, now, is fully open—nothing.

Just be this.

What is a Holiday?

It's not about getting a little awareness or anything like that.

A Holiday is the end of everything—
it's the end of your entire life story.

Look now and see.

Your life story is not actual, is it?

The story of you, this character, is it actual?

Look, be honest.

A Holiday is the death of the character of you.

All the "poor me" stories,
all the "great me" stories,
all the remorse and regret,
all the nostalgia and sentimentality,
are any of those true?

Look, be honest.

We have been believing in fairytales.

We go into those fairytales hoping for some resolution,
hoping to find some peace, hoping to find happiness,
but it is an endless and fruitless search.

Peace and freedom are found in what's true, what actually is.

Look, be honest.

If thoughts appear about some story,
those thoughts are appearing now, but the
actual events and experiences the thoughts are referring to,
where are they now?

Are they here?

So then, you can disregard them.

Be no one.

This is being nothing.

This is truth.

Thoughts come and go, it's normal. There's nothing we can do about thoughts coming and going. That's the job of the brain, recording the experiences that happen throughout the course of life and then playing them back as thought. There's no problem with this and nothing to do about it.

The problem is we think thoughts/stories have value and we have to do something "in there," we have to get rid of them, resolve them, refine them, purify them, understand them, transcend them, etc. No, it is just a natural function of the brain, recording and playing back experiences.

There is no inherent value to that.

So disregard, ignore. Disregard the stories the brain is throwing up. Ignore them as they are not true, they are not you.

The only thing you can't deny,
the only thing that's actually true, is

I am, here and now.

Here and now is who you are.

You = Here.

You = Now.

Be who you are.

This is freedom.

You don't have to get rid of thoughts or do anything with them. There is nothing wrong with them. There is nothing wrong with anything. Whatever appears is appearing. So, it is right, not wrong! Placing inordinate value on whatever appears is what causes confusion and suffering.

All psychology, philosophy and spirituality is arguing with what's appearing. It is trying to understand, change, purify or get rid of what's appearing. Instead of arguing, just turn attention to freedom. Be free, be nothing.

You don't have to worry about getting rid of anything, purifying your mind or working with your vasanas. It's a relief.

How could you possibly deal with all of that anyway? It's no wonder they tell you it will take fifty lifetimes. How about looking now and seeing what's true instead?

There are no vasanas.
There is nothing that needs fifty lifetimes to purify.

This is good news.

The only time freedom is, is now.
It is not available in the future.
There is no future.

It's here, now.

Freedom is only, ever, always now!

Be free.

Notice the complete infatuation with whatever comes up in the mind and
the thinking that there's something important in there.
It's just cultural ignorance that conditions us to think this.

Notice what's important, truth.

Have freedom now.
Have it now.
Have it now.

Holidays are not a means to an end.
You don't have a Holiday so that you'll be free one day.

A Holiday is to be free, now.

It is the end itself.

On Holiday, you see that you are free, now.

Now, in this moment, it's over.

This work is not about seeking.

There is nothing more to seek.
There is nothing more to seek.
There is nothing more to seek.

It's about being finished, now.
It's about living freedom, now.

You are it.

Be honest and see,
do you want nothing?

Mainly, we still want something.
It is normal and habitual to want something more—
more experiences, more understanding or more states.

We don't want nothing.

Recognize this.

Look, here and now,
there's no seeking, it is finished now.

Then notice the mind wants something
but, but, but, but, but, but, but. . . .
What about this, what about that?
This teacher said this, that teacher said that.
This book said this, that book said that.

It's all mind.

Stop and look again, now.

Nothing.

Recognize the wanting of something.

Don't attempt to get rid of wanting something.
Just see that it's a habit of mind, nothing else.

Then again, have a Holiday.
See, here and now is nothing—freedom.

What's true is freedom.

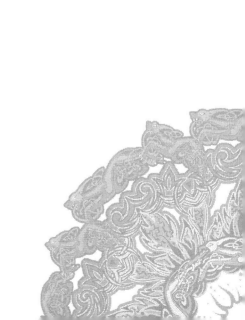

YOU GET NOTHING

ENLIGHTENMENT IS A VERY BIG WORD. So, we believe
it can't be simple and obvious, it has to be something very
grandiose, but let's look.

Relax the focus of attention so that you are not
attending to anything in particular,
any thoughts, sights, sounds or sensations.

Just know that you're here.

Just be here knowing nothing.
Just be here, now.
No past.
No future.

Only this.

What if you found out that all of
your ideas about enlightenment, liberation, spirituality,
non-duality, advaita, attachment and non-attachment,
transcendental states, surrender, etc.
meant absolutely nothing?

What if you just found yourself, here and now,
knowing none of that at all
and getting none of it?

What if you found out that your entire library of spiritual
books was only good kindling for starting fires?

What if you found out that you,
ordinary you, just as you are,
are the big enlightenment that you've heard about?

What if you found out that the long, yellow-brick road
of spirituality you've been walking on all these years, that's
been leading you to all the gurus behind curtains,
was a complete waste of time, meaningless and got you
nowhere?

What if you found out that this huge, enormous
desire to be the special enlightened one
is completely meaningless and you get nothing?

You get to be you—ordinary, this.

How would you like that?

Right now, here.
Just here.

Right now is freedom.
This is freedom, here and now.

This is it.

The mind, which has been filled with nonsense your whole life,
is the only thing that says, this is not it.

One needs to have the eyes to see,
and then you will see.

This is it.

ANYTHING OTHER THAN NOTHING, IS THOUGHT

FREEDOM IS TO LIVE, IT'S NOT TO ATTAIN. You don't attain freedom, you don't attain liberation, you come to know it and then live it. It's life, that's what it is, life. You have your bumps, pains and pleasures along the way, like everyone. The human body goes through whatever it goes through, no problem. It doesn't mean anything.

I watch the news and see all of the lunacy in the world and I'm amazed by it, but I have to be honest, what do I know about what's right or wrong? Let's step back from the planet earth and look at it from Mars. What do we actually know from this vantage point? Maybe all the events I consider to be lunacy are not bad, maybe they are good, maybe they need to happen.

I'm not making a statement that it has to happen or not. What I'm saying is, how do I know? I don't know. I know in my own life, often the worst things that ever happened turned out to be the best things that ever happened. The things that made me suffer and brought me to my knees were the things that woke me up. If we broaden our perspective and go a few light-years away from earth, then what's happening right now? Just the reshuffling of a few atoms— nothing.

This is what most people don't want. Most people want to think they know what's right, clench their fists and shout out at people who don't agree with them (i.e. politics).

It's okay, just see what's true.

Come back again to knowing nothing, freedom.

Here I am.

Just . . .

No words.

If you want truth, freedom,
you have to be free of everything,
including knowing the "right way" things have to be.

You are no-thing.

You have nothing,
you know nothing and
you are nothing.

This is freedom.

Anything other than nothing,
is thought.

Anything,
anything,
anything other
than nothing is thought.

If you want freedom,
it's not found in thought.
The answer isn't there.

Recognize freedom,
and then live free, that's all.

Living free is not trivial. There is a lifetime of ignorance and one has to be devoted to truth to be free. Continuing to be on Holiday makes a big impact.

Removing your head is the easy part. Habitually, picking it back up and putting it back on isgoing to happen, no problem. Just remove it again. Pick it up, put it back on, and remove it again. That's all.

FREEDOM, A BREATH OF FRESH AIR

Let's just be here together, for real.

Be who you are—knowing.

Here, there are no nationalities, genders, social classes,
castes, job descriptions or political affiliations.

Here, there are no identities like mother, father, brother, sister.
Here, there is no one who is enlightened or unenlightened.
Here, there is no teacher or student.

Past and future don't exist and there are
no personal stories.

What's left?

You, you are left.

Everything you think you are
is changing, constantly.

The body is constantly changing,
without one second of stagnation.
Thoughts, beliefs, concepts, desires
and fears are all changing.

Feelings change,
friends and family change,
living arrangements change
and health changes.

Everything changes, even the sex of the body can change.

Throughout all of this, what doesn't change?

Anything that is something, you can and will lose.

You can lose your loved ones,
you can lose your house,
you can lose your job,
you can lose your sight,
you can lose the ability to function, etc.

Throughout your entire life, all experiences come and go,
none of them are permanent.

Everything goes, everything you've ever had is gone,
there's no exception.
Look and see,
how many things have come and gone in your life?

And, in a moment of loss, you can be inconsolable.
It's true for everyone.

But, look now.
What have you actually lost?

Something is lost right now?
Something is missing?

You've lost everything and yet, you are perfectly fine, now.

You've lost everything you've ever had,
you will continue to lose everything,
and you are always fine.

Look, now.

So then, what's valuable?
The things you believe you have?

They will be gone, no exceptions.

They are already on the way out,
so how valuable are they?

Is your peace in things—
the relationship,
the job,
the house, etc.?

Is your contentment in things?

Is your fulfillment in things?

They are all going.

What can you always rely on?
What is always whole and complete?

What is always at rest?
What is always fulfilled?

You, you are.

Value what's actually true.

Value what is already complete, whole and fulfilled.
Value your own essential nature, freedom.

If that's your highest value, you're fine.

Look.

You can't lose yourself.

So, be that which has never changed, now.

Be yourself.

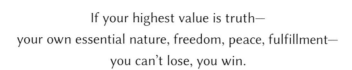

If your highest value is truth—
your own essential nature, freedom, peace, fulfillment—
you can't lose, you win.

So, what do you value?

If your highest value is money
and you lose the money, then you are a mess.
If your highest value is a relationship
and you lose the relationship, then you're a mess.

Everything you've lost means nothing, now.

See for yourself.

This is what freedom is.

Freedom is the complete reconciliation with the fact
that every appearance is coming and going.
Nothing is substantial or eternal about
any appearance, nothing.

The only thing that is eternal is you.
When this is reconciled, there is peace.

There is peace in the midst of constant change.
There is peace in the midst of loss.

Recognize freedom and the simple truth—
everything comes and everything goes, nothing stays, nothing.

The more that reconciliation is here,
the more you see the profound nature of freedom.

You know the joy of
having nothing,
knowing nothing and
being nothing.

Here,
the pathology of fearing loss and desiring things to remain the same,
the incessant clutching and holding on to things,
is not.

Here,
that pathology ends.

In freedom, we can enjoy all the great things and
we can feel the pain of all the terrible things.

When it's here, it's here and when it's gone, it's gone.

That's it, and you remain.

This is fulfillment.
This is peace.
This is freedom.

When you recognize freedom,
you have a big breath of fresh air.

Everything is always coming and going and you are completely fine.

See the power in this way of being,
the joy, happiness, contentment and peace.

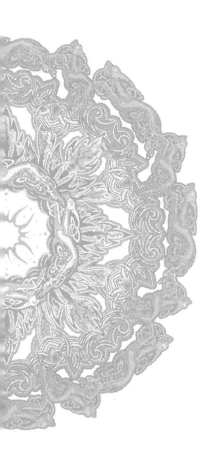

UNCONDITIONAL LOVE

This, who you are,
free, unborn and aware,
is all-inclusive.

It excludes nothing.

It is complete, unconditional inclusion.
This complete, unconditional inclusion, is love.

When you hear about unconditional love,
you think it means you, the perceiver,
loving an object, unconditionally.

But the true unconditional love is all-inclusive knowing.

Who you are is free, unborn, aware,
and so is everyone else.

And, within everyone,
everything is included,
unconditionally.

LOVE!!

NOTHING TO HOLD
ON TO

When we want to know what's true,
we get honest and stop lying to ourselves and
we see there is no such thing as the past or future.

You can see this for yourself, now.

Look.

What exists is this,
this is existent.

Past and future are concepts.
They do not exist.

Since the past does not exist, what happens
to all of your poor me and great me stories?

Those are just myths, aren't they?

If you want to get real and be honest,
it doesn't matter how bad or how great
they appear to be, there is no truth to any of them.

It also doesn't matter what you think, hope
or fear will happen in the future.

Those are just fantasies.
There's no truth to them.

Truth is only this, now.

This is true.

Right now, you can say,
I know I am.

I AM, I EXIST.

The knowing I am pointing to
is not thought,
it is not intellectual.

It's knowing.

It's only now.

There's no knowing in the so-called past or future.

Knowing is always and only now.

Whatever is appearing now is in constant flux.
It is ephemeral, not substantial, changing constantly.

It is an appearance, it is not actual.

Whatever you think appeared in the so-called past is not true
because where is it now?

Whatever you think will appear in the so-called future is not true
because where is it now?

Whatever is appearing now,
a sight,
a sound,
a thought,
a sensation,
is true as an appearance only.

Appearances are not true as solidified, actual, independent objects.
Everything is in constant flux, every moment, every millisecond.

There's nothing to hold on to.

What is happening now is not a million different things.
What is happening now is one.

This now moment is all-inclusive.

The mind breaks it up into
this thought and that feeling
and this object and that object.

In truth,
in knowing,
there is only one thing happening, now.

It's all one knowing, now.

Knowing knows this one moment,
this one fleeting, ephemeral moment.

This moment is in constant flux like a wave in the ocean.

Wave is an appearance,
which is coming and going in ocean.

Wave is completely ephemeral,
there's nothing stagnant,
nothing solid.

Not for one billionth of a millisecond is wave stagnant.
It is in constant change the whole time of its appearance
until it's gone.

Yet, wave is always ocean.
Wave is always water.

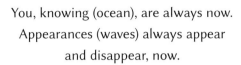

You, knowing (ocean), are always now.
Appearances (waves) always appear
and disappear, now.

WHAT IF THERE WERE
NO WORDS

Be here, knowing.

Most of our existence is spent in words.
The words running around as thoughts
in the mind and the spoken words.

We have a whole world created by words
and it is just going on in the mind all the time.

What if there were no words?

What if there was nothing?

The words you are reading are here to point,
but then they have to be abandoned.

The most fundamental word I use to point is

Knowing.

Then that word can go.

NOW IS ALWAYS
THE BEGINNING

IF YOU KNOW THERE'S WATER IN THIS HOLE, then keep digging here. If you start digging other holes, then you'll never get to the water.

You know there's water because you recognize, here and now. Let's just see it again.

Obviously, there's only now, and
this aware knowing is present, knowing itself.

Where is the past?
Where is the future?

Clearly, it's only now.

If we're being honest,
there's no past and no future, is there?

This is very simple,
extremely simple, and very stark.

There is no past and there is no future.

So then, where is the self?

The self-story, the one with a past/future,
doesn't exist, it's a myth.

Let's get real, there's only now.
It's very stark.

I heard someone say that freedom has no history.
I say, "*You* have no history."

You are only now.

You and now are the same.

You are not *in* the now, you are now.

You = Now.

This is jumping off all of it.

It's jumping off everything.

Everything we've believed ourselves to be
and have been affected and victimized by is all gone.

A mature person is ready for this—
to be reconciled with the fact that there is only now.

A mature person isn't a victim
any longer of past myths and future fantasies.

This is the beginning, knowing this.

This is the beginning and we're always at the beginning.

This is it.

I'm free.

The full reconciliation that this, now, is it,
is the resolution of all doubts.

What we see now is the beginning,

but reconciliation takes time

because we've been indoctrinated with bad habits.

We have been taught—
go in there,
believe that thought,
believe that story,
believe that myth,
believe that fantasy . . .

It's like this for everyone,
and it takes time for these habits to end.

So, keep having Holidays,
see what's true,
again see what's true,
again see what's true . . .

BE HOME

Your essential being is free—Here, Now, Always.

This is true.

Your infatuation with time, which is self,
keeps you from knowing what is so obvious.

It keeps you from reconciling with the simplicity of truth,
which you are.

You always want something—more, less, special,
past, future, becoming, relief, bliss, etc.

This desire for something keeps you on the carousel of self,
of me, of suffering forever.

Want only what is true—what you actually know.

No new state,
no transcendence of your humanity,
no enlightenment and
no liberation.

Simply, what is true, now.

What do I actually know, now?

Who am I, now?

Be finished with your "me" story.
Jump, here and now.

Be home.

Home,
where you have always been
and have never left.

BLOWN WIDE OPEN

Let's come to recognize something,
not by using the mind, but by knowing.

The way it works is to allow your attention to be wide open,
not focused on anything in particular.

Some thoughts or sounds may come. This is all perfectly fine,
but when you notice that you are attending to anything in particular,
allow attention to be blown wide open, here and now—

just for a moment.

Be relaxed, keep your eyes open
and allow attention to be wide open.

Again, maybe some thoughts will come,
and attention will go to those thoughts,
that is not a problem.

When you notice attention is going to thoughts,
in the noticing itself, attention relaxes.

When attention relaxes, see that your natural
condition is blown wide open.

What is, is fully open knowing, here and now.

Knowing no particular object, but instead,
blown wide open knowing, in which all objects are included.

The sounds, smells, visions and sensations of the body—
everything is included in blown wide open knowing.

When attention focuses on one thing, especially strong thoughts,
you see that it becomes very exclusive, contracted and limited.

Your experience becomes very contracted and limited,
and that one object becomes the main thing, the only thing.

But when you relax from that, and are blown wide open,
you see that everything is included here.

This work is just about being honest,
and seeing what is actually true, and what is not true.

What's true is, here and now is all that actually is.

What's not true, not actual, is something called a past.

Just be honest, look and see,
is there a past?

Does past exist?

Just be honest, look and see,
is there a future?

Does future exist?

What actually is?

Get real, there is only now.

Do you have a name, a gender, a particular nationality
or any other characteristics?
Look.

If you say you have any of these, what are you referring to?
You are referring to thoughts.

So, for a moment, don't refer to thoughts.

Simply be here now,
wide open, knowing.

Is there any name, gender or nationality to this?

Aren't you only
here and now?

You are not *in* the now, you *are* now.

Since there is no past, then what about all the other
stories you have been believing about who you are?

All the regrets, the guilts, the remorses, the great me, the poor me,
the traumatized me, the historical me,
where are any of them now?

Look now, does any of that exist?

Just be honest.

Freedom is about getting real.
And what's real is, you have no history.

If you want to get real, then you have to admit . . .
I HAVE NO HISTORY!

If you believe you are the mind, then you will say you have a history.

You have been referring to mind as who you are, your whole life.

Now, have a shift of knowing, know yourself in a different way—
not as mind, but as no-thing, free of history.

If a thought comes up, referring to a past, no problem.
There is nothing wrong with anything, including a *thought* of a so-called past.

But if you want freedom, in the moment that you notice a thought is happening
and you are referring to yourself as that thought, get real—
be blown wide open, knowing.

See that you are actually no-thing.

See that you have no history,
FREE!

All of your sadhanas (spiritual practices) to attain something in the future,
to be something other than you are now, are all, and only, mind!

No sadhana is needed to know who you are.

Another 20 years of meditating will not bring you one step closer
to who you are because you are already who you are.

Know who you are, now.

You are free, here and now.

All of the sadhanas that promise something in the future,
are rendered false and pointless when you discover that there is no future.

When will you get enlightened?
In the future?

When are you going to recognize your essential nature,
the Self, with a capital S?
In the future?

What about now?

Simply know, I.
And see, here and now, I am free already.

Be blown wide open, knowing.

This is a completely different knowing.

It is not knowing an object, separate from itself.
It is knowing, knowing itself.

It is you knowing yourself—
I—I.

I know I am.

This knowing is also being.
Knowing who you are equals being who you are.
KnowingBeing.

When you *know* who you are, you *are* who you are. So, just be yourself.

I am.

This is not a sadhana, it is not a practice.

It is simply knowing, immediately, that you are free,
and being that, now.

Now and now and now . . .

You have spent a lifetime of seeking,
not just spiritual seeking, but mundane seeking as well:
to be different than what you are;
to improve what you are;
to get more and more things; and
to attain enlightenment.

This movement of seeking more and more has been your entire life,
and it will continue on its own until,
in the moment of noticing that movement,
you are blown wide open knowing, you are free, now
and there is nothing to attain.

You see you are already free.

The movement of seeking is the movement of trying to be
something other than what you actually are.

It is the movement *away* from truth, not *towards* truth.

For a moment, be who you are, blown wide open,
no past, no future, no history,
nothing.

And know, I am free, here and now.
Full stop!

Is nothing enough?

Existing not as something: a mind, a body, a seeker or a nationality,
but simply being, here and now—

BLOWN WIDE OPEN

I know that I am!

For someone who wants freedom, the answer is, Yes!

You are wide open, knowing.

There is nothing to attain.
So relax, there is no need to look
for peace or bliss or a silent mind . . .

Simply be who you are, knowingly.

Be Blown Wide Open, knowingly.

This is a Holiday.

Be free!

OTHER BOOKS BY SALVADORE POE

Liberation IS, The End of the Spiritual Path

The Way of Freedom. Conversations with Salvadore Poe

AVAILABLE ON AMAZON AND INGRAMSPARK

10 Day Intensives in Tiruvannamalai, India

For information:

http://www.liberationis.com/intensives/

Online Open Meetings on Zoom

http://www.liberationis.com/open-meetings/

FOR MORE:

http://www.liberationis.com/

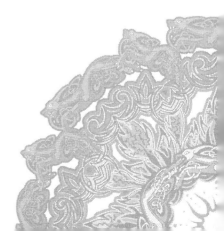

Made in the USA
Columbia, SC
23 September 2020

21391532R00212